A PLUME BOOK

TAKE ME WITH YOU

© MORGAN SCHUER

ANDREA GIBSON IS ONE OF THE MOST QUOTABLE AND INFLUENTIAL POETS OF OUR TIME AND HAS MADE A CAREER AT THE FOREFRONT OF THE SPOKEN WORD MOVEMENT. GIBSON (THEY/THEM) REGULARLY TOURS, PERFORMING POETRY THAT FOCUSES ON GENDER NORMS, POLITICS, SOCIAL REFORM, AND THE STRUGGLES LGBTQ PEOPLE FACE IN TODAY'S SOCIETY. A DEVOTED FAN BASE SEES GIBSON'S WORK AS A RALLY CRY FOR ACTION AND A WELCOME MAT AT THE DOOR OF THE HEART'S MOST COMPASSIONATE ROOM. BORN IN CALAIS, MAINE, GIBSON NOW RESIDES OUTSIDE BOULDER, COLORADO.

TAKE ME WITH YOU

ANDREA GIBSON

PLUME

PLUME
AN IMPRINT OF PENGUIN RANDOM HOUSE LLC
375 HUDSON STREET
NEW YORK, NEW YORK 10014

COPYRIGHT © 2018 BY ANDREA GIBSON

ILLUSTRATIONS BY SARAH J. COLEMAN

LIBRARY OF CONGRESS CATALOGING-IN-PUBLICATION DATA
NAMES: GIBSON, ANDREA (POET), AUTHOR.
TITLE: TAKE ME WITH YOU / ANDREA GIBSON.
DESCRIPTION: FIRST EDITION. | NEW YORK: PLUME, 2018.
IDENTIFIERS: LCCN 2017024213 (PRINT) | LCCN 2017035119 (EBOOK) |
ISBN 9780735219526 (EBOOK) | ISBN 9780735219519 (PAPERBACK)
SUBJECTS: LCSH: LESBIANS—POETRY. | BISAC: POETRY / AMERICAN / GENERAL.
CLASSIFICATION: LCC PS3607.I2638 (EBOOK) |
LCC PS3607.I2638 .A6 2018 (PRINT)
| DDC 811/.6—DC23
LC RECORD AVAILABLE AT HTTPS://LCCN.LOC.GOV/2017024213

PRINTED IN THE UNITED STATES OF AMERICA

3 5 7 9 10 8 6 4 2

BOOK DESIGN BY FINE DESIGN

For my family,
which includes
you,
dear reader

TAKE ME
WITH YOU

1

ON LOVE

WHENEVER,
HOWEVER,
THIS ENDS,
I WANT YOU TO KNOW
THAT RIGHT NOW,

I LOVE YOU
FOREVER.

RIGHT
NOW.

FOREVER.

3

JUST TO BE CLEAR, I DON'T
WANT TO GET OUT WITHOUT A
BROKEN HEART.
I INTEND
TO LEAVE
THIS LIFE SO
SHATTERED
THERE
BETTER BE A
THOUSAND SEPARATE HEAVENS FOR
ALL MY FLYING PARTS.

IF LOVE DID NOT EXIST
I WOULD BE SO GODDAMN SANE.

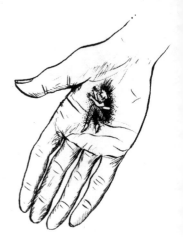

MAYBE

I NEED YOU THE
WAY THAT BIG
MOON NEEDS THAT
OPEN SEA.

MAYBE I DIDN'T EVEN KNOW I WAS

HERE 'TIL I SAW YOU
HOLDING ME.
GIVE ME ONE ROOM TO COME HOME TO.
GIVE ME THE PALM OF YOUR HAND.

HAS YOUR HEART
EVER BEEN A
HOARDER?

MINE HAS.
BUT MOSTLY I DON'T KEEP
ANYTHING
BUT MY WORD.

I HAVE NEVER MADE A LOVE
POTION THAT HASN'T BLOWN UP.

TODAY IN THE GROCERY STORE I
FOUND ONE OF YOUR HAIRS
IN MY UNDERWEAR.
I PULLED IT OUT IN THE FROZEN
FOOD SECTION AND SCREAMED,

"THAT IS SO GORGEOUS
IT COULD KILL A MAN."

GOOD THING I'M
A LEPRECHAUN.
LUCKY, LUCKY.

IT TAKES GUTS TO TREMBLE. IT TAKES SO MUCH TREMBLE TO LOVE, EVERY FIRST DATE IS AN EARTHQUAKE.

I MASTERED THE ART OF CROCHET AND I
CROCHETED HER A WINTER SCARF
AND ONE NIGHT AT THE BAR I GAVE IT TO
HER WITH A NOTE THAT SAID SOMETHING
LIKE "I HOPE THIS KEEPS YOUR NECK
WARM. IF IT DOESN'T, GIVE ME A CALL."
THE KEY TO FINDING LOVE IS MESSING UP
THE PATTERN ON PURPOSE,
IS SKIPPING A STITCH, IS LEAVING A
TINY, TINY HOLE TO LET THE COLD IN
AND HOPING SHE MENDS IT WITH
YOUR LIPS.

YOU
WILL
NEVER
HAVE
TO
LOSE
YOURSELF
TO
WIN
ME
OVER.

DO YOU KNOW THE NIGHT YOU TOLD
ME YOU HAVE A CRUSH ON MY EARS I
SWORE TO NEVER BECOME VAN GOGH?

(AND LOOK. THEY'RE BOTH STILL HERE.)

SHE'S A METAL POLE IN
ZERO-DEGREE WEATHER.
I'M AFRAID IF I PUT MY
TONGUE
ON HER, IT
WILL STICK
FOREVER.

I WILL

NEVER

MAKE A

PIÑATA

OF YOUR

HEART.

THIS MORNING I SAW
HER LIPSTICK ON A
COFFEE CUP AND FELT
LIKE I HAD NEVER
KNOWN A BRUISE.

SHE MAKES ME FEEL LIKE
I COULD WIN THE LOTTERY
WITH A PARKING TICKET.

IF YOU SEE HER,

TELL HER THE MOON

IS ALL HER FAULT.

BEFORE I MET YOU

MY JOY HAD SUCH AN

EARLY CURFEW

IT DIDN'T BOTHER GOING OUT.

YOU HAVE TO UNDERSTAND, WHEN IT
HURT TO LOVE HER,
IT HURT THE WAY THE LIGHT HURTS
YOUR EYES IN THE MIDDLE
OF THE NIGHT.

BUT I HAD TO SEE.

I DON'T CARE ABOUT ANY
OF THE WORDS ON THE MAP
BESIDES

YOU ARE HERE.

RIGHT NOW SHE'S SLEEPING BESIDE
ME, MAKING A FACE SHE WOULD
NOT WANT TO KNOW
SHE'S MAKING.

CALL IT THE OPPOSITE OF HER
MIRROR FACE. CALL IT ME
BRINGING HOME THE GOLD.

YOU LOOK LIKE MARILYN MONROE AND IT

MAKES ME WANNA RUN . . . FOR PRESIDENT.

She STILL asks for my number every time we kiss. STILL stops me from carving our initials into the tree, whispering,

"EVERYTHING THAT GROWS ALREADY KNOWS WHO WE ARE."

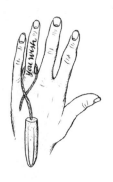

YOU HAVE A FRIEND WHO TATTOOED THE
WORDS "YOU WISH" ON HER RING
FINGER. I HAVE A FRIEND WHO PULLED
OUT HER TAMPON ON THE STREETS
OF MANHATTAN AND THREW IT AT A
MISOGYNIST COP.
WE'RE PERFECT FOR EACH OTHER.

I'M NEVER GONNA WAIT THAT
EXTRA TWENTY MINUTES TO
TEXT YOU BACK AND I'M NEVER
GONNA PLAY HARD TO GET.

I KNOW YOUR LIFE HAS BEEN
HARD ENOUGH ALREADY.

I KNOW THE EXACT LOOK ON HER FACE THE FIRST TIME SHE USED MY TOOTHBRUSH. THE NEXT DAY I BRUSHED MY TEETH AT LEAST THIRTY TIMES SO I WOULDN'T HAVE TO LET HER GO.

I KNOW HOW MUCH THE
PAIN OF THIS WORLD
WEIGHS BUT I CAN
STILL TIP THE SCALES
IN LIGHT'S DIRECTION
WHENEVER I HAVE
YOUR NAME ON MY
TONGUE.

WHEN THE ASTRONAUT TOLD ME SHE
NEEDED MORE SPACE, I DROPPED MY
PANTS TO THE FLOOR IN THE GROCERY
STORE, HOPING I COULD MOON HER
INTO STAYING.

WE WEAR OUR TRAUMAS
THE WAY THE
GUILLOTINE WEARS
GRAVITY.

OUR LOVERS' NECKS ARE SO SOFT.

IT TAKES A HELL OF

A LOT MORE MUSCLE

TO STAY

THAN TO GO.

I LOVED YOU FROM OUR FIRST DATE
AT THE BATTING CAGES WHEN I
MISSED TWENTY-THREE BALLS IN A
ROW AND YOU LOOKED AT ME LIKE
I WAS A HOME RUN IN THE NINTH
INNING OF THE WORLD SERIES. NOW
EVERY TIME I HEAR THE WORD "LOVE"
I THINK, "GOING, GOING . . ."

IN THE GHOST TOWN OF OUR
LOVE THERE IS A PLAYER PIANO
TRYING TO PROVE IT CAN MAKE
MUSIC WITHOUT BEING TOUCHED.
MY FINGERTIPS MISS HER SO MUCH.

I WISH I WAS THE PHOTOGRAPH
IN YOUR WALLET.

I WISH I WAS THE FACE YOU SHOW
TO STRANGERS WHEN THEY ASK WHERE
YOU COME FROM.

I SWEAR TO GOD IF I HAD AN
ADAM'S APPLE,
I'D TELL HER TO PEEL IT
AND TAKE A BITE.

I DON'T WANT TO WRITE ONE
MORE POEM ABOUT PEACE 'TIL
I'VE FIGURED OUT HOW TO SEW
A WHITE FLAG OUT OF OUR
BEDSHEETS.

surrender

AS FOR MY HEART
I'LL SAY:
A MUSIC BOX IS
STILL A MUSIC BOX
EVEN WHEN IT'S
CLOSED.

IF THE TOOTH FAIRY HADN'T COME ANY
OF THOSE TIMES, I'D GIVE HER MY
SMILE AND SAY,
"YOU'RE THE REASON
WHY I'M GAY,"
AND I MEAN THAT THE OLD-FASHIONED
WAY, AS IN HAPPY,
BUT ALSO THE OTHER WAY TOO.

WHEN THEY ASK WHY WE STAYED
TOGETHER FOR SO LONG I SAY,
"I DON'T KNOW. I JUST KNOW THAT
WE CRIED AT THE EXACT SAME TIME
IN EVERY MOVIE.

"I KNOW WE BLUSHED EVERY DAY FOR
THE FIRST TWO YEARS.

"I KNOW I ALWAYS STOLE THE COVERS
AND SHE NEVER WOKE ME UP."

I'VE FINALLY LEARNED
LOVE PRAYS IT WON'T
ALWAYS LIVE PAYCHECK
TO PAYCHECK.
BUT IT ALWAYS DOES,
EVEN WHEN IT'S GOT
FOREVER ON ITS LIPS.

LOVE,

I KNOW IT IS NOT SEXY TO
MAKE OUT WITH SOMEONE WHO
CONSTANTLY HAS THEIR FOOT IN
THEIR MOUTH.

I KNOW THERE ARE COUPLES WHO NEVER ARGUE. BUT YOU AND I, WE ARE ALWAYS GOING TO FIGHT FOR LOVE.

 I BOUGHT A TYPEWRITER WHEN WE SAID GOOD-BYE, HOPING TO MAKE A LIFE I COULDN'T ERASE SO EASILY THE NEXT TIME.

LIKE
PAC-MAN,
SHE SWALLOWS
MY GHOSTS.

AUTUMN

IS THE HARDEST SEASON.

THE LEAVES ARE FALLING LIKE

THEY'RE FALLING IN LOVE

WITH THE GROUND.

I'M NOT A PESSIMIST, I'M JUST THINKING
ABOUT HOW SHE SAID, "I LOVE YOU,"
WHILE I WAS HAVING A PANIC ATTACK
AND HOW THAT MEANS SHE'S PROBABLY
A LIAR AND HOW SHE'LL LIKELY CUT
OFF HER OWN NOSE TO PROVE ME WRONG
AND HOW THEN SHE WON'T SMELL MY
PHEROMONES AND HOW THEN WE'LL BOTH
DIE OF LESBIAN BED DEATH.

MY HEART IS STILL A
LETTER JACKET

I AM WAITING TO GIVE TO
SOMEONE SWEET.

I WOULD GIVE HER MY NAME, BUT
I'D RATHER HAVE HERS SO WHEN THE
TELEMARKETERS CALL AND SAY, "WITH
WHOM AM I SPEAKING?" I COULD SAY IT
ALOUD, THE NAME I WAS BORN WITH BUT
DIDN'T KNOW UNTIL I WIPED THE SWEAT
OFF HER ARMS ON A DANCE FLOOR IN
OAKLAND, THEN LICKED HER SALT OFF THE
LENGTH OF MY HAND. DO YOU UNDERSTAND
HOW SICK A PERSON GETS LICKING THEIR
HANDS IN A NIGHTCLUB? I DIDN'T LEAVE
THE BATHROOM FOR SEVEN DAYS, WHICH
IS TO SAY I WANT TO GIVE HER MY TIME,
MY DECADES EVEN.

MY FIREFLY HEART IS STILL RIGHT
THERE IN YOUR GLASS JAR.
I NEVER TRUSTED ANYBODY MORE TO
POKE ENOUGH HOLES IN THE LID.

I KNOW SOME PEOPLE
BUILD THEIR SAFETY
WITH WALLS. ME,
I'M INTO DEMOLITION—
WHATEVER TEARS THE
WALLS DOWN.

I HAVE A HARD TIME
KISSING WITHOUT THAT KIND OF DUST IN
THE AIR.
I SEE A WRECKING BALL AND SEE A
WEDDING RING, THINK,

"LOOK AT THE SIZE OF
THAT STONE."

ASK ME TO GIVE YOU
EVERYTHING I HAVE,
KNOWING I'LL GIVE YOU MY WORD
THAT IF YOU FALL IN THE FOREST
WHEN THERE'S NO ONE AROUND
I'LL BE THERE BEFORE YOU LAND.

YOU WANT TO HEAR THE BEST STORY YOU'VE
EVER HEARD IN YOUR LIFE?
I MET A WOMAN AND WE WERE LYING IN HER
BED, ABOUT TO KISS FOR THE VERY FIRST TIME.
JUST BEFORE OUR LIPS TOUCHED SHE JUMPED
UP AND RAN TO HER CLOSET AND GRABBED A
STETHOSCOPE. SHE CAME BACK TO THE BED,
PUT THE EARPIECES IN MY EARS, SLIPPED THE
DISC DOWN HER SHIRT ONTO HER HEART, AND
WHISPERED, "I WANT YOU TO LISTEN TO MY
HEART SPEED UP WHEN YOU KISS ME." AND I
KISSED HER, AND I LISTENED TO HER HEART
BEAT FASTER AND FASTER AND FASTER.

MORAL OF THE STORY: BUY A STETHOSCOPE.

YOU ALREADY KNOW HOW
MANY POEMS
I HAVE WRITTEN FOR WOMEN
WHO WERE NOT YOU.

YOU ALREADY KNOW
EVERY WORD WAS TRUE.

I DON'T STILL HAVE THE RING
YOU GAVE ME.

I CRUSHED IT WITH A ROCK TO
SEE HOW MUCH YOU LOVED ME.

I LOVE YOU TO PIECES TOO.

DARLING, WHEN I GAVE YOU MY
HEART I GAVE MY LIFE MY WORD
THAT IT WOULD NOT BE THE SAME
HEART I HAD GIVEN BEFORE. I PUT
IN LIKE A HUNDRED MORE DOORS
AND A RECORD PLAYER FROM A REAL
RECORD STORE. I PUT IN A
SKYLIGHT THAT IS ALL YOURS
THE DAY YOU PICKED ME UP AND
CARRIED ME THROUGH THAT AIRPORT
LIKE MY GOOD-BYE HAD NO WEIGHT.
MY GOOD-BYE HAS NO WEIGHT.

I FIND GREAT COMFORT IN
BELIEVING ANYONE WHO HAS EVER
BROKEN UP
WITH ME HAS
PROBABLY
NEVER GOTTEN
OVER MY DOG.

THAT'S HOW I WAS LIVING:
DECADES OF *NO NO NO NO NO NO
NO NO NO*. AND THAT'S OKAY, AN
ACCORDION CANNOT MAKE A SONG IF
IT NEVER CLOSES. BUT THEN I MET YOU
AND I STARTED FEELING MYSELF OPEN,
STARTED FEELING MY *YES* COMING BACK
AND IT WAS THE SWEETEST THING I'D
EVER KNOWN. IT WAS THE REVERSE
OF BEING HAUNTED, LIKE TAKING A
DEEP BREATH AND PULLING THE FOG
OFF THE GLASS. MY LOVE, MY YES, DO
YOU KNOW HOW MANY TIMES A DAY MY
GRATITUDE FRAMES YOUR AUTOGRAPH?

THERE WAS A TYPO IN THE BOOK.
THE LINE READ,

"I WANT TO MERRY YOU."

I THOUGHT, "THAT'S EXACTLY WHAT I
WANT TO DO: *MERRY* SOMEBODY."

MY LOVE,

COME BECOME BESIDE ME, 'TIL I FIND

YOUR FIRST SILVER HAIR IN OUR TUB.

'TIL I FIND YOUR LAST SILVER

HAIR IN OUR TUB.

BEFORE I DIE, I WANT TO BE
SOMEBODY'S FAVORITE HIDING
PLACE, THE PLACE THEY CAN PUT
EVERYTHING THEY KNOW THEY
NEED TO SURVIVE, EVERY SECRET,
EVERY SOLITUDE, EVERY NERVOUS
PRAYER, AND BE ABSOLUTELY
CERTAIN I WILL KEEP IT SAFE.

I WILL KEEP IT SAFE.

11
ON THE WORLD

WE
HAVE
TO
CREATE.

IT IS THE ONLY THING
LOUDER THAN DESTRUCTION.

THE TRAUMA SAID,
"DON'T WRITE THIS POEM.
NOBODY WANTS TO HEAR YOU CRY ABOUT
THE GRIEF INSIDE YOUR BONES."
BUT MY BONES SAID,
"REMEMBER THE BOY WHO DOVE INTO
THE HUDSON RIVER CONVINCED HE WAS
ENTIRELY ALONE."
MY BONES SAID, "WRITE THE POEM."

I AM SO DESPERATE TO LEARN
HOW PEOPLE REACH
EACH OTHER,
I CAN'T STOP RUNNING
AROUND CURSING THIS CITY
FOR THE DAY THEY STARTED
BURYING THE TELEPHONE WIRES
UNDERGROUND.

THE TEACHER SAID,
"SILENCE IS GOLDEN."

I SAID,
"SILENCE IS BRONZE
AT BEST."

I STOPPED CALLING MYSELF
A PACIFIST WHEN I HEARD
GANDHI TOLD WOMEN THEY
SHOULD NOT PHYSICALLY FIGHT
OFF THEIR RAPISTS.

I BELIEVE THERE IS SUCH A
THING AS A NONVIOLENT FIST.

"SIR. SIR. DO YOU REALIZE
THIS IS THE LADIES' ROOM?!"
"YES, MA'AM, I DO.
IT'S JUST I DIDN'T FEEL
COMFORTABLE
STICKING THIS
TAMPON UP MY
PENIS IN THE MEN'S
ROOM."

ANY FEMINIST WHO HAS EVER TAKEN
THE HIGH ROAD WILL TELL YOU THE
HIGH ROAD GETS BACKED UP AND
SOMETIMES WE NEED TO TAKE A DETOUR
STRAIGHT THROUGH THE BELLY OF
UNCENSORED RAGE.

ONCE

I FOUND A BUTTERFLY'S WING ON
THE SIDEWALK.
I WANTED TO KEEP IT BUT I DIDN'T. I
KNEW THERE WERE THINGS I SHOULD NEVER
FIND BEAUTIFUL.
LIKE DEATH.
AND GIRLS.

WHAT I QUESTION IS THE IDEA OF
HEAVEN HAVING GATES—SILLY.

LAST SPRING, ON TOUR, A FRIEND TOLD ME THAT NINA SIMONE SPENT SEVERAL YEARS DURING THE CIVIL RIGHTS MOVEMENT REFUSING TO SING LOVE SONGS, REFUSING TO SING ANYTHING BUT SONGS FOR JUSTICE AND CHANGE. WHEN I HEARD THAT, I FELT SO CHARGED AND INSPIRED. HOW FIERCE. HOW POWERFUL. HOW RELENTLESSLY COMMITTED. THAT NIGHT, BEFORE I GOT ONSTAGE, I HAD THE THOUGHT THAT I WASN'T GOING TO READ A SINGLE LOVE POEM. I DECIDED I WAS GOING TO READ ONLY SOCIAL JUSTICE POETRY THROUGH MY ENTIRE SET. BUT WHEN I WAS MAKING MY SET LIST IT HIT ME THAT THE SIMPLE EXISTENCE OF THE WORD "SHE" IN MY LOVE POEM MADE IT A POLITICAL POEM. ISN'T THAT CRIMINAL?

ISN'T IT CRIMINAL THAT LOVE IS A POLITICAL THING? THAT THE HEART IS A POLITICAL THING?

I VISITED A MEN'S PRISON AND
WHEN I WAS LEAVING, THE SNOW
STARTED FALLING ON THE BARBED-
WIRE FENCE AND I LOOKED BACK
TO SEE IF THERE WERE FACES
WATCHING IT FROM THE WINDOWS.
BUT THERE WERE NO WINDOWS.

AMERICA: HOME OF THE BRAVE HATE.
LAND OF THE PRISON BARS
PASSING AS PIANO KEYS, GENOCIDE.

MUSIC IN THE EARS OF WHITE FOLKS
WHO BELIEVED THE BLUES
WERE FOR THEM, RAISED THEIR
CHILDREN TO TAKE WHAT WASN'T
THEIRS,

TO CALL IT POLITENESS
WHEN THEY UNRAVELED THE NOOSE
AND ASKED IF THEY COULD TOUCH
THE DEAD'S HAIR.

OUR INSANITY ISN'T THAT WE SEE
PEOPLE WHO AREN'T REALLY THERE.
IT'S THAT WE IGNORE THE ONES
WHO ARE.

SAFETY ISN'T ALWAYS SAFE.

YOU CAN FIND ONE ON EVERY GUN.

I AM AIMING TO DO BETTER.

I TELL MY LOVER THERE IS A BIBLE ON
MY BOOKSHELF I NEED HER TO SMACK ME
WITH. THERE IS AN ANCHOR I AM STILL
PULLING UP TO FREE ALL THE PARTS OF
MYSELF FLOATING ON NOAH'S ARK. RIGHT
BETWEEN THE ZEBRAS AND THE PENGUINS,
MY KINK SIDE IS CURLED UP IN A BALL,
BITING ITS CLAWS, BEGGING THE RAIN TO
STOP. YOU SHOULD NEVER TRUST A SHIP
THAT WON'T LET YOU GET OFF.

I KNOW GOD'S NUMBER BY
HEART.

I KNOW IT ISN'T LISTED IN
ANY BOOK.

I WANT TO DEMAND THAT LUCK
NOT BE THE THING THAT KEEPS US
ALIVE. I WANT TO STOKE THE HOLY
FIRE OF MY OWN IMPATIENCE AND
BURN THE WORD "TOLERANCE."
TOLERANCE IS A MURDERER.

 TOLERANCE SHINES
THE BULLET.

NO TOLERANT PERSON OR SYSTEM OF
GOVERNMENT IS AN ADVOCATE FOR
LOVE OR LIFE OR PEACE.

THE WOMAN BEHIND THE COUNTER LOOKS
UP FROM HER NAIL FILE AND TELLS ME
THAT I AM ONE "ADORABLE LITTLE BOY."
ON THE CAR RIDE HOME I THINK OF THE
LITANY OF THINGS WE WILL DO TO FIX

ME. THAT NIGHT AFTER
DINNER I DIG TO THE
BOTTOM OF MY FIRE-RED
TOY BOX 'TIL I FIND
THE DOLL WITH THE
GOLDEN HAIR. I CRADLE
HER IN MY ARMS AND
WAIT TO BE SEEN. I
DECIDE LOVE IS A SILENT AUCTION AND I
AM WORTH MORE SOLD.

BURY ME IN A
BLUE BLANKET
SO THEIR GOD
DOESN'T KNOW
I'M A GIRL.
CUT OFF MY
CURLS.
I WANT PEACE
WHEN I'M DEAD.

I WORE A FLOWERED DRESS TO
MY BIRTHDAY BOY PARTY.
DON'T LOOK AT ME LIKE THAT.
I'M NOT THE BOX THE GIFT
CAME IN.

WHAT IF THE WEATHER KEEPS
CHANGING AND WE DON'T?

WHEN A WAR ENDS, WHAT DOES
THAT LOOK LIKE EXACTLY?

DO THE CELLS IN THE BODY
STOP DETONATING THEMSELVES?

DOES THE ORPHANAGE STOP
SCREAMING FOR ITS MOTHER?

WE WERE ALL BORN ON DAYS
WHEN TOO MANY PEOPLE
DIED IN TERRIBLE WAYS,
BUT YOU STILL HAVE TO
CALL IT A BIRTHDAY.

PROMISE THAT WHO WE
WEEP AND FIGHT AND
TEAR DOWN THE SUN
FOR WILL NOT ONLY
BE OUR OWN FACES IN
THE MIRROR.

I'D BE LYING IF I SAID I'M
NOT TERRIFIED OF BEING SEEN
WITHOUT MY WISDOM TEETH,
WORRYING ABOUT MY HAIR EVERY
TIME EMPATHY HAS BEEN
OVER MY HEAD.

THERE IS
NO WEAPON
MORE
DANGEROUS
THAN A
WOUND.

WAKE ME
WHEN THE
AMERICAN
DREAM IS
OVER.

THAT I COMMIT TO A LIFE OF OPENING AND
LEARNING, THAT I COMMIT TO LEARNING AT A
SPEED THAT IS VIGILANT AND AWAKE, THAT
I COMMIT TO KNOWING WHERE MY EMPATHIES
LEAN AND WHY THEY LEAN THERE, THAT I
BECOME INCREASINGLY FAMILIAR WITH THE
WHY OF WHAT RAISES MY VOICE, THAT I
BECOME INCREASINGLY FAMILIAR WITH THE
WHY OF WHAT LULLS ME TO SILENCE, THAT
I BE HAUNTED BY THE GHOSTS OF WHO MY
SILENCES HAVE HARMED, THAT I ACKNOWLEDGE
THAT HAUNTING IS NOT AN UNKINDNESS, THAT
I ACKNOWLEDGE THAT HAUNTING IS LOVE,
THAT I TRUST LOVE LIVES IN WHATEVER POINTS
AT THE DARK, THAT I ACKNOWLEDGE THAT
SHAME IS RARELY THE SEED OF COMPASSION,
THAT I ACKNOWLEDGE SHAME WOULD LIKELY BE
MY LAZIEST GESTURE, THAT I STOP DENYING
I AM A WHOLE PERSON, AND MY WHOLENESS

IS OFTEN UNLOVABLE, AND MY WHOLENESS IS
OFTEN LOVABLE, THAT I OWN THE POSSIBILITY
THAT THERE ISN'T A THING ONE COULD SAY
ABOUT THE PERSON I AM THAT I COULD
WHOLEHEARTEDLY DENY, ALL OF IT—YES, ALL
OF THE UGLY—YES, ALL OF THE BEAUTY—
YES, I HAVE FAILED AND WILL
CONTINUE TO FAIL,

I HAVE LOVED AND WILL CONTINUE TO
LOVE, I AM COMMITTED TO LEARNING AND
OPENING, I WANT PEOPLE AROUND ME WHO ARE
COMMITTED TO LEARNING AND OPENING, PEOPLE
WHO ARE FAILING AND LOVING, PEOPLE WHO
ARE STALKING THEIR OWN VIGILANCE, THE
SPEED OF THEIR OWN COMPASSION, SAYING,

"FASTER FASTER FASTER."

WHO WITH A HEART
CAN STOMACH HOW
MUCH THEY CAN
STOMACH?

THROW
BACK
THE
TEAR
GAS.

THEY WANT YOU THINKING YOU'RE
BAD AT BEING A GIRL INSTEAD OF
THINKING YOU'RE GOOD AT BEING
YOURSELF. THEY WANT YOU TO BUY
YOUR BLUSH FROM A STORE INSTEAD
OF LETTING IT BLOOM FROM YOUR
BUTTERFLIES. THEY'RE TELLING YOU
TO BLEND IN, LIKE YOU'VE NEVER
SEEN HOW A BLENDER WORKS, LIKE
THEY THINK YOU'VE
NEVER SEEN THE MESS
FROM THE BLADE.

I KNOW DAVID ARGUED WITH THE CHISEL. I KNOW HE SAID, "MAKE ME SOFTER."

SHE'S NOT ASKING WHAT YOU'RE GONNA TELL YOUR DAUGHTER. SHE'S ASKING WHAT YOU'RE GONNA TEACH YOUR SON.

WOMAN, ARE YOU A CARBON COPY
OF MYSELF? IS THERE A BOY INSIDE
YOU PAINTING YOUR CELLS WITH THE
CHARCOAL OF CINDERED FEATHERS SO YOU
WILL NEVER AGAIN GLOW IN THE DARK
THE WAY GIRLS DO?

WE HAVE THE NERVE
TO *SUPPORT OUR
TROOPS* WITH PRETTY
YELLOW RIBBONS WHILE
GIVING NOTHING BUT
DIRTY LOOKS TO THEIR
OUTSTRETCHED HANDS.

A SEA
OF BLOOD,
AMERICA,
AND NOT
EVEN A
SHELL HELD
TO YOUR EAR.

I GREW UP IN THE TOWN THAT RECEIVED
THE FIRST DISTRESS SIGNAL SAYING THE
TITANIC WAS GOING DOWN. IT WAS THE
ONLY THING WE WERE EVER RENOWNED
FOR. IN FACT, WE PRIDED OURSELVES ON

OUR FAILURE
TO SAVE THE
SINKING, WHICH
IS MAYBE PART
OF THE REASON
I PRIDED
MYSELF ON

DRINKING MY FIRST FIFTH OF WHISKEY AT
TWELVE YEARS OLD. IT'S COLD WHERE I
COME FROM. I LEARNED TO DROWN YOUNG.

PATRIARCHY
TAUGHT ME HOW TO
TAKE A PUNCH
BETTER THAN I
COULD TAKE A
COMPLIMENT.

I SHOVEL MY BLOOD FROM
THE WHITE SNOW, I WIPE
MY FRANTIC BREATH FROM
THE WINDOW, AND BIND
MY BREASTS SO THAT
SOMETHING WILL HOLD
MY BREATH SO TIGHT NOT
EVEN THE AIR IN MY LUNGS
COULD BE IDENTIFIED AS
WOMAN.

EVEN WHEN THE TRUTH
ISN'T HOPEFUL,
THE TELLING OF IT IS.

I SMASHED MY MASON JAR AND
THREW AWAY THE LID.

I DIDN'T WANT TO TAKE A CHANCE
THAT I'D GROW UP TO BE A WAR.

I WONDER
HOW MANY PEOPLE HAVE DIED
DRIVING WHILE CHECKING

HOW MANY LIKES
THEIR FACEBOOK STATUS GOT.
I WONDER HOW MUCH LIFE
HAS BEEN LOST IN
THE BLOODY DITCH
OF APPROVAL,

HOW MANY
SKULLS
HAVE SWALLOWED WINDSHIELDS
TRYING TO SEE IF THEY ARE
WORTHY OF APPLAUSE, WORTHY
OF THEIR OWN HEART'S HUNGRY BEAT.

NOTHING HURTS MORE THAN LIVING SOMEONE ELSE'S LIFE.

MY FIRST PSYCHOTHERAPIST TOLD ME
TO SPEND THREE HOURS EACH DAY
SITTING IN A DARK CLOSET WITH MY
EYES CLOSED AND MY EARS PLUGGED.
I TRIED IT ONCE BUT COULDN'T STOP
THINKING HOW GAY IT WAS TO BE
SITTING IN THE CLOSET.

REMEMBER THE TIME WHEN WE SAW TWO
BOYS KISSING ON THE STREET IN KANSAS
AND WE BOTH BROKE DOWN CRYING,
'CAUSE IT WAS KANSAS, AND YOU SAID,

"WHAT ARE THE CHANCES
OF SEEING ANYTHING BUT
CORN IN KANSAS?!"

WE WERE BORN AGAIN THAT DAY. I CUT
YOUR CORD AND YOU CUT MINE.

OH, STOP HATING ON LOVE.

WHY BE THE VACCINE FOR
GOOSEBUMPS?

I KNOW A THOUSAND
THINGS LOUDER THAN
A SOLDIER'S GUN.

I KNOW THE
HEARTBEAT OF HIS
MOTHER.

I KEEP REMEMBERING BEING
FIFTEEN AT DISNEYLAND
WEARING MY BEST FRIEND'S
HOODIE LIKE IT WAS MY
BOYFRIEND'S CLASS RING. HOW
MANY YEARS IT TOOK ME JUST
TO TOUCH HER FACE. HOW MANY
YEARS I SPENT PRAYING MY
HEART COULD PLAY DEAD 'TIL
THE THREAT WAS GONE, 'TIL THE
WORLD CHANGED, 'TIL HISTORY
WAS HISTORY.

IN GYM CLASS, A GIRL CALLED ME
A DYKE AND I DIDN'T HAVE THE
LANGUAGE TO TELL HER SHE WAS
WRONG AND RIGHT. I JUST SHOWED UP
AT HER HOUSE PROMISING TO PAINT
MY FINGERNAILS RED WITH WHAT
WOULD GUSH FROM HER BUSTED FACE
IF SHE EVER SAID IT AGAIN.

IT'S A MYTH THAT
KIDS ARE CRUEL,
BECAUSE WE
DON'T GROW OUT
OF IT.

I AM THE ONLY BOY
I EVER WANTED TO
TEAR MY DRESS
OFF FOR.

I KNOW EVERY
BELT THAT HAS HIT
SOMEONE'S BACK IS
STILL A BELT THAT
WAS BUILT TO
HOLD SOMETHING
UP.

I EXPLAIN MY GENDER BY
SAYING I AM HAPPIEST ON
THE ROAD WHEN I'M NOT
HERE OR THERE, BUT
IN BETWEEN, THAT
YELLOW LINE COMING
DOWN THE CENTER OF IT
ALL LIKE A GODDAMN
SUNBEAM.

WHEN THE FIRST RESPONDERS ENTERED THE PULSE
NIGHTCLUB AFTER THE MASSACRE IN ORLANDO,
THEY WALKED THROUGH THE HORRIFIC SCENE OF
BODIES AND CALLED OUT,
"IF YOU'RE ALIVE, RAISE YOUR HAND." I WAS
SLEEPING IN A HOTEL IN THE MIDWEST AT THE
TIME BUT I IMAGINE IN THAT EXACT MOMENT MY
HAND TWITCHED IN MY SLEEP—
SOME UNCONSCIOUS PART OF ME
AWARE THAT I HAD A PULSE,
THAT I WAS ALIVE.

IT'S TRUE WHAT THEY SAY
ABOUT THE GAYS BEING SO
FASHIONABLE, OUR GHOSTS

NEVER GO
OUT OF
STYLE. EVEN
LIFE IS LIKE
FUNERAL
PRACTICE,

HALF OF US ALREADY DEAD
TO OUR FAMILIES BEFORE WE
DIE. HALF OF US STILL ON OUR
KNEES TRYING TO CRAWL INTO
THE FAMILY PHOTO.

I BECAME A
VEGETARIAN
THE YEAR OF MY
FATHER'S FIRST
HEART ATTACK.

I WANT TO LIVE
A HUNDRED YEARS ON
WHAT I REFUSE TO KILL.

THIS IS FOR THE TIMES YOU WENT
THROUGH HELL SO THAT SOMEONE
ELSE WOULDN'T HAVE TO.

COMING INTO OUR OWN HUMANITY OFTEN TAKES
ENORMOUS EFFORT, COMMITMENT, AND BRAVERY. I
BELIEVE WE SHOULD BE TAUGHT THAT AT AN EARLY
AGE. I BELIEVE PART OF THE VIOLENCE OF OUR
CULTURE STIRS FROM THE MYTH THAT KINDNESS IS
NATURAL. I DON'T THINK KINDNESS IS NATURAL.
I THINK KINDNESS WOULD ONLY BE NATURAL IN A
WORLD WHERE NO ONE IS HURT, AND EVERYONE IS

HURT. SO KINDNESS IS
WORK. KINDNESS IS OUR
KNEES IN THE GARDEN
WEEDING OUR BITES,
OUR APATHIES, OUR
COLD SHOULDERS, OUR SILENCES, OUR CRUELTIES,
WHATEVER TAUGHT
US THE WORD "UGLY."

WHEN ASKED IF I BELIEVE IN "GOOD PEOPLE," I SAY I BELIEVE IN PEOPLE WHO ARE COMMITTED TO KNOWING THEIR OWN WOUNDS INTIMATELY. PEOPLE WHO READ THEIR WOUNDS' DIARIES, WHO FOLLOW THEIR WOUNDS OUT WINDOWS, DOWN LADDERS, ASKING, "WHERE ARE YOU GOING? WHAT DO YOU NEED? HOW CAN I INTERVENE BEFORE A CRUEL THING IS DONE OR SAID?"

I AM
SO GRATEFUL
FOR HAVING
A MIND THAT
CAN BE CHANGED.

AMERICA WAKES ME IN THE MIDDLE OF
THE NIGHT, TELLS ME SHE HAD A BAD
DREAM, ONE WHERE THE BOOTSTRAPS HUNG
FROM TREES, ONE WHERE THE MORGUE
PINNED FLOWERS ON PROM SUITS, ONE
WHERE THE CASKET WAS A FULL STOMACH
GROWLING FOR MORE. IN THE DREAM,
AMERICA FINALLY ELECTED A PRESIDENT
WHO TOLD THE TRUTH, WHO DIDN'T BOTHER
WEARING A SHEET, WHO KNEW HIS SHOES
WOULD BE RECOGNIZED ON WALL STREET.
IN THE DREAM, THE SCALES OF JUSTICE
WERE BUSY DISCUSSING MISS AMERICA'S
WEIGHT.

AND ALL THEY KNOW OF

HATE IS THAT IT COULDN'T

BEAT THE LOVE OUT OF

ME.

I CRIED IN A CLOUD OF
TEAR GAS AT A PEACEFUL
PROTEST. I DECIDED I WAS
TOO SOFT TO LAST,
AND THEN I DECIDED TO BE
SOFTER.

III
ON BECOMING

A DOCTOR ONCE
TOLD ME I FEEL TOO
MUCH. I SAID,
"SO DOES GOD.
THAT'S WHY YOU
CAN SEE THE
GRAND CANYON
FROM THE MOON."

FEELINGS
ARE
NOT
THE
ENEMY.

BEATING YOURSELF UP IS NEVER A FAIR FIGHT.

ALL LIVING IS STORM
CHASING. EVERY GOOD HEART
HAS LOST ITS ROOF. LET THE
WALLS COLLAPSE AT YOUR
FEET. SCREAM, "*TIMBER*"
WHEN THEY ASK HOW YOU
ARE. "FINE" IS THE SUCKIEST
WORD. IT IS THE OPPOSITE OF
"HERE."

FOR HALLOWEEN I'M GOING TO BE
"EMOTIONALLY STABLE." NO ONE
IS GOING TO KNOW IT'S ME.

139

EVEN AFTER ALL THIS THERAPY, I'M STILL NOT RIGHT IN THE HEAD. GUESS I'M ALWAYS GONNA BE A LEFTY.

I ASK YOU ABOUT BEING HAPPY THE
SAME WAY MY HIGH SCHOOL FRIENDS
ASK ME ABOUT BEING GAY.
"SO WHAT DO YOU
PEOPLE DO EXACTLY?
I MEAN, HOW DO YOU
DO IT?"

I KEEP WAITING TO GET
HIGH ON LIFE.
I KEEP WAITING TO WAKE
UP IN A FIELD
REMEMBERING I SPENT THE
WHOLE NIGHT
SNORTING THE LINES THE
PLANES LEFT IN THE SKY,
MY BLOODSTREAM FULL OF
HONEYMOONS.

THE FIRST TIME I CAME OUT, I CAME OUT TO MY ROOMMATE IN MY CATHOLIC DORM. I'D JUST COME FROM A SCIENCE CLASS THAT WAS TAUGHT BY A NUN WHO, NO JOKE, DIDN'T BELIEVE IN DINOSAURS. WE WERE SITTING ON MY BED. I DIDN'T SAY THE WORDS "GAY" OR "QUEER." I LOOKED AT MY FRIEND AND SAID, "I GOTTA TELL YOU SOMETHING. I FINALLY UNDERSTAND GOD . . ."

WHAT I KNOW ABOUT
LIVING IS THAT THE
PAIN IS NEVER JUST
OURS. EVERY TIME
I HURT I KNOW THE
WOUND IS AN ECHO, SO
I KEEP LISTENING FOR
THE MOMENT THE GRIEF
BECOMES A WINDOW,
WHEN I CAN SEE WHAT I
COULDN'T SEE BEFORE.

I TOLD MYSELF I WAS BUILT
LIKE A DRUM.

I WOULDN'T MAKE A SONG IF
I'D NEVER BEEN HIT.

IT WAS A DESPERATE THEORY.

TODAY AT THE GROCERY STORE A WOMAN
STOPPED IN HER TRACKS AND REFUSED TO
WALK BESIDE ME DOWN THE STAIRWAY,
SAYING (AND I SWEAR THIS IS TRUE),
"I DON'T WANT TO WALK NEXT TO YOU
BECAUSE YOU'RE GAY." I THINK IT WAS THE
SIMPLE FACT OF IT THAT STUNNED ME MORE
THAN SOME INTENDED INSULT SCREAMED OUT
OF A CAR WINDOW MIGHT HAVE STUNNED
ME. MY HEART HAS BEEN RATTLED ALL DAY
BECAUSE OF IT, AND THEN I SAW THIS
TREE, THIS BEAUTIFUL, BEAUTIFUL TREE,
AND I WANT TO FIND A SHOVEL, AND FIND
THAT WOMAN'S HOUSE, AND PLANT THIS
TREE IN HER FRONT YARD WHILE SHE'S
SLEEPING, AND I WANT HER TO WAKE TO
THE BLOOM OF IT, SMILING, AND I WANT NO
ONE BUT GOD TO TELL HER WHO IT'S FROM.

146

BITTERNESS IS HELL.
I'VE BEEN WORKING MY ASH OFF.

YOU
ARE
NOT
WEAK
JUST
BECAUSE
YOUR
HEART
FEELS
SO
HEAVY.

ONLY I KNOW HOW BROKE I GOT
BUYING INTO THE THEORY THAT MY
LIFE WAS SOMETHING
THAT HAPPENED TO ME.
AND THAT'S NOT TO SAY I GAVE
EVERY HURT A PERMISSION SLIP.
I DIDN'T. BUT I DID CAST MYSELF IN
A LOT OF CRAPPY ROLES. I'VE BEEN
TOLD ALMOST EVERY ARGUMENT IS A
RACE FOR THE VICTIM POSITION. I'M
TIRED OF WINNING THE GOLD.

JUST ME AND MY SUITCASE,
HANGING OUT WITH THE SUN,
LEARNING HOW TO PACK LIGHT.

MY MOTHER USED TO KNIT MY MITTENS
TOO BIG SO THEY'D STILL FIT ME WHEN
I GREW. I WORE THEM AND I'D LOOK
LIKE WHAT I WASN'T YET. I FEEL THAT
SOMETIMES WHEN I'M WRITING POEMS,
THEY DON'T YET FIT. EVER FEEL LIKE
THE BEST OF YOU IS SOMETHING YOU'RE
STILL HOPING TO GROW INTO?

IF YOU'VE NEVER HAD A PANIC
ATTACK, THERE'S A GOOD CHANCE
YOU'VE BEEN AN ASS TO SOMEONE
WHO HAS. IT MAKES SENSE THAT
"JUST RELAX" WOULD FEEL LIKE A
HELPFUL THING TO SAY IF OXYGEN
HAS NEVER BEEN OVER YOUR
HEAD, IF YOUR BODY HAS NEVER
BECOME ITS OWN CORSET CINCHING
YOUR LUNGS INTO SOMETHING
YOU IMAGINE LOOKS LIKE A
USED CONDOM BENEATH THE PARK
BENCH. I'M SCREWED EVEN WHEN I
MEDITATE.

I WONDER HOW
MUCH OF MY TIME
I SPEND BUILDING
BOMB SHELTERS TO
KEEP THIS LIFE FROM
BLOWING MY MIND.

I THINK MAYBE THE
STARS I SAW THE
FIRST TIME I WAS
PUNCHED ARE THE
SAME STARS I SAW
THE FIRST TIME I WAS
KISSED AND I CAN
FIND MY WAY HOME BY
ALL OF IT.

I HOPE NEVER TO BE AN
HONEST POET.

I HOPE TO ALWAYS
FORGIVE FASTER THAN I
WRITE.

I WONDER IF BEETHOVEN HELD HIS
BREATH THE FIRST TIME HIS FINGERS
TOUCHED THE KEYS, THE SAME WAY
A SOLDIER HOLDS HIS BREATH THE
FIRST TIME HIS FINGER CLICKS THE
TRIGGER. WE ALL HAVE DIFFERENT
REASONS FOR FORGETTING TO
BREATHE.

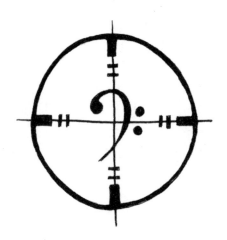

I WATCHED A DANDELION
LOSE ITS MIND IN THE
WIND AND WHEN IT DID IT
SCATTERED A THOUSAND
SEEDS, SO THE NEXT TIME
I TELL YOU I'M COMING
OUT OF MY SKIN, DON'T
TRY TO PUT ME BACK IN.

I SUPPOSE I LOVE
THIS LIFE.
IN SPITE OF MY CLENCHED FIST.

WHEN I'M HAVING A PANIC ATTACK AND CAN'T BREATHE, I TELL MYSELF, "THAT ISN'T THE DEVIL CLUTCHING MY WINDPIPE WITH A PITCHFORK! THAT'S GOD REMEMBERING I'VE ALWAYS WANTED AN ADAM'S APPLE AND THERE GO THE ANGELS PLANTING THE ORCHARD IN MY THROAT!"

I DO NOT NEED AIR
TRAFFIC CONTROL TO
TELL ME THERE MAY
NEVER BE ENOUGH
FLIGHTS FOR ME TO LOSE
ALL OF MY BAGGAGE.

YOU KEEP REMEMBERING THE
FIRST TIME YOU SAW A BIRD'S
NEST HELD TOGETHER BY AN OLD
SHOELACE AND SCRAPS OF A
PLASTIC BAG. YOU KNEW THE HOME
OF A PERSON COULD BE BUILT LIKE
THAT—A LOT OF THINGS YOU'D
RATHER THROW AWAY.

I DON'T CONSIDER MYSELF A COLD PERSON, BUT THERE'S THAT WINDCHILL FACTOR.

I WANT TO BREAK

EVERY PROMISE

I HAVE MADE

TO MY PAIN.

THIS YEAR EVERYONE I KNOW HAD A BROKEN HEART. EVERYONE I KNOW CRIED IN PRIVATE ON THEIR WAY HOME FROM A PARTY, AND NOT EVERYONE I KNOW WOKE UP THE NEXT MORNING, AND NOT EVERYONE I KNOW WANTED TO EVEN THOUGH THEY DID. AND THIS YEAR I STOOD INSIDE OF A REDWOOD TREE AND THOUGHT, "THIS IS THE SWEETEST DAY OF MY WHOLE LIFE," AND TWO MONTHS LATER I WAS SOBBING IN A PARKING LOT, THINKING, "THIS IS THE WORST DAY OF MY WHOLE LIFE," AND A FEW MONTHS LATER I WAS DANCING IN MY LIVING ROOM, SAYING, "THIS IS THE BEST DAY OF MY WHOLE . . ." HAVE YOU EVER SEEN THE SEED OF A REDWOOD TREE? SO TINY. AND ALL OF THAT EVERYTHING INSIDE OF IT. ALL OF THIS EVERYTHING INSIDE OF US.

THE WORST THING THAT EVER
HAPPENED TO ME
WAS NOT THE WORST THING
THAT EVER HAPPENED TO ME.
HATING MYSELF FOR IT WAS.

COMMIT TO
LOVING YOURSELF
COMPLETELY.

IT'S THE MOST RADICAL
THING YOU WILL DO IN
YOUR LIFETIME.

THANK GOD YOU NEVER
GOT BRACES.
YOUR BITE LOOKS LIKE A
CITY SKYLINE.

I BET YOU'LL LEAVE THAT
KIND OF MARK ON
THIS WORLD.

I THINK EVERY GOOD ARTIST MAKES
THEIR AUDIENCE UNCOMFORTABLE. I'D
HOPED TO DO THAT WITH MY POLITICS
AND NOT MY ANXIETY FLAILING
LIKE THE ABOUT-TO-BE-DEAD GIRL
IN A TEENAGE HORROR FLICK, NOT
MY SWEAT SALTING MY CONFIDENCE
LIKE A SLAB OF MEAT FOR A PACK
OF RABID COYOTES, MY OWN SPINE
CURLING INTO THE CLAW THAT
STRIPS ME DOWN TO MY DAY-OF-THE-
WEEK PANTIES—AND IT'S ALWAYS
DOOMSDAY.

I SAID TO THE SUN,
"TELL ME ABOUT THE
BIG BANG."

THE SUN SAID,
"IT HURTS TO BECOME."

SCIENCE JUST PROVED THAT AN
ATOM CAN EXIST IN TWO PLACES
AT ONE TIME AND I BELIEVE
PEOPLE ARE NOT ALWAYS ONLY
AT THE SCENE OF THEIR CRIMES.
EVEN THE WORST OF US, I TRUST,
ARE OFTEN ALSO SOMEWHERE HOLY,
SOMEWHERE KIND.

I'M SITTING ON MY FRIEND'S COUCH SEVERAL
MONTHS INTO BEING INTENTIONALLY SINGLE
AND CELIBATE FOR THE FIRST TIME SINCE I
WAS TWENTY YEARS OLD. I'M TELLING MY
FRIEND ABOUT THE PSYCHIC WHO SAID I'M
GONNA MEET THE LOVE OF MY LIFE BY THE
END OF JANUARY. IT'S JANUARY TENTH AND
I AM SO FAR FROM READY FOR CUPID, THAT
NAKED LITTLE SHIT, TO FIRE ANYTHING SHARP
MY WAY. SO FAR FROM READY TO BE THE KIND
OF INSANE ONLY LOVE MAKES ME. MY FRIEND
MUSTERS EVERY BIT OF NEW AGE JARGON
SHE CAN FIT ONTO HER TONGUE AND SAYS,
"WHAT IF YOU ARE THE LOVE OF YOUR LIFE?"
I THINK, "OH MY GOD, I HOPE THAT'S NOT
TRUE . . . BECAUSE I AM ABSOLUTELY
NOT MY TYPE."

MY PANIC GOOGLED,
"HOW TO
PERFORM CPR ON
YOURSELF."

IT'S TWO A.M. THE EMERGENCY ROOM
PSYCHIATRIST LOOKS UP FROM HIS
CLIPBOARD WITH EYES PAID TO CARE AND
ASKS ME IF I SEE PEOPLE WHO "AREN'T
REALLY THERE." I SAY, "I SEE PEOPLE,
HOW THE HELL AM I SUPPOSED TO KNOW
IF THEY'RE *REALLY THERE* OR NOT?"

THE DAY YOU DIED
BECAUSE YOU WANTED
TO, I TIED MY WISDOM
TOOTH TO A DOORKNOB
AND PULLED IT LOOSE.
TAKE EVERYTHING I THINK
I KNOW. EVERY ANSWER
IS A GRAVE. EVERY QUESTION IS RAIN I
WALK THROUGH NOW TO FIND MY WAY TO
GOD, AND MY ONLY GOD IS FAITH THAT
THERE IS COMFORT HERE, THAT WHO IS
HURTING WILL HURT LESS THAN THEY DID
BEFORE.

IF ONLY SHAME COULD
WASH ME CLEAN,
BUT THAT IS NEVER
HOW HEALING WORKS.
NOBODY EVER WON
ANYTHING FROM ANYONE
THINKING THE WHOLE
WORLD WAS OUT OF
THEIR LEAGUE.

I AM ALREADY BUILDING
A MUSEUM FOR EVERY
TREASURE YOU UNEARTH IN
THE ROCK BOTTOM.

SOME PEOPLE HOLLER
INTO THE CANYON
AND HEAR SOMEONE
ELSE'S VOICE
ECHOING BACK.
DON'T LET THAT BE
YOUR LIFE.

FORESTS MAY BE
GORGEOUS BUT THERE
IS NOTHING MORE ALIVE
THAN A TREE THAT
GROWS IN A CEMETERY.

EVERYBODY'S
DARK
SIDE
IS
DAYTIME
SOMEWHERE.

THE HARDEST PEOPLE IN THE WORLD TO FORGIVE ARE THE PEOPLE WE ONCE WERE. THE PEOPLE WE ARE TRYING DESPERATELY TO NOT STIR INTO THE RECIPE OF WHO WE ARE NOW.

I IMAGINE WHAT THE FLOWER
WANTED TO SAY TO THE FIRST
HUMAN TRYING TO NAME HALF
ITS PETALS LOVE ME NOTS:

"NO. THAT IS NOT HOW
ANYTHING GROWS."

I GET ONLINE TWENTY TIMES
A DAY FOR THE SOLE PURPOSE
OF MAKING SURE I HAVE NOT
ACCIDENTALLY POSTED A NUDE
PHOTO OF MYSELF.

BRAVE

IS A HAND-ME-DOWN SUIT FROM

TERRIFIED AS HELL.

SOME PEOPLE WILL NEVER
UNDERSTAND THE KIND OF
SUPERPOWER IT TAKES FOR SOME
PEOPLE TO JUST WALK OUTSIDE.

WHY ISN'T IT OKAY
TO SAY THERE ARE
THINGS WE HAVE
NOT SURVIVED?

YOU KEEP WORRYING
YOU'RE TAKING UP
TOO MUCH SPACE.
I WISH YOU'D LET
YOURSELF BE THE
MILKY WAY.

I COULDN'T TAKE A
COMPLIMENT WITHOUT
FEELING LIKE A THIEF,
COULDN'T BELIEVE ANYTHING
PAST THE FIRST PAGE OF ME
WAS WORTH THE READ.

IT WAS A LIE.

PICTURE THE 738 SELFIES I DELETED
BEFORE I TOOK ONE I WAS WILLING
TO SHOW TO THE WORLD. PICTURE
ME WISHING I COULD GET ALL OF
THEM BACK—MY SO-CALLED FLAWS
STACKED LIKE BASEBALL CARDS I
KNOW WILL BE WORTH SOMETHING
SOMEDAY.

I DON'T WANT TO BE
BEAUTIFUL,
I WANT WHAT
EVERYONE WANTS:

TO BE
BEAUTIFUL,
UGLY,
AND
LOVED.

I'M NINE YEARS OLD. I DON'T
YET KNOW MY NAME IS A SONG
I WON'T ALWAYS SING UNDER
MY BREATH. I DON'T KNOW MY
PRONOUNS HAVEN'T EVEN BEEN
INVENTED YET. I DON'T KNOW I'M
GOING TO SHAVE MY HEAD AND
DRIVE THROUGH TEXAS. I'M GOING
TO KILL MY OWN GOD TO FALL IN
LOVE FOR THE FIRST TIME.

YOU ARE
THE BEST
THING
THAT HAS
EVER
HAPPENED
TO YOU.

IT'S OKAY.
EVERYBODY'S
SURVIVAL LOOKS
A LITTLE BIT LIKE
DEATH SOMETIMES.

WHAT I WANT MOST IS TO LIVE THE REST OF MY LIFE DESPERATELY WANTING TO LIVE IT. I WANT TO GIVE THAT TO YOU. I WANT YOU TO BELIEVE IT IS SOMETHING. WHEN I SAY I WANT TO MAKE SOMETHING OF MY LIFE, THAT'S WHAT I MEAN.

REMEMBER THAT PHOTOGRAPH OF YOU AT FIVE YEARS OLD, FROM THE YEAR YOU RAN AWAY FROM SCHOOL BECAUSE YOU WANTED TO GO HOME?

YOU ARE ALMOST THERE.

"See you soon!" 1986

LET ME SAY RIGHT NOW FOR THE RECORD: I'M STILL GONNA BE HERE ASKING THIS WORLD TO DANCE. EVEN IF IT KEEPS STEPPING ON MY HOLY FEET. YOU, YOU STAY HERE WITH ME, OKAY? YOU STAY HERE WITH ME. RAISING YOUR BITE AGAINST THE BITTER DARK, YOUR BRIGHT LONGING, YOUR BRILLIANT FIST OF LOSS. FRIEND, IF THE ONLY THING WE HAVE TO GAIN IN STAYING IS EACH OTHER, MY GOD THAT IS PLENTY. MY GOD THAT IS ENOUGH. MY GOD THAT IS SO, SO MUCH FOR THE LIGHT TO GIVE. EACH OF US AT EACH OTHER'S BACKS WHISPERING OVER AND OVER AND OVER,

"LIVE. LIVE. LIVE."

ACKNOWLEDGMENTS

THANK YOU TO MEGAN FALLEY,
WHOSE SUPPORT, ENCOURAGEMENT,
AND WILLINGNESS TO READ THROUGH
TWO DECADES OF LOVE POEMS PULLED
THIS BOOK INTO BEING.

WRITEBLOODY
QUALITY AMERICAN BOOKS